DRAW ANIMALS

in **4** Easy Steps

Then Write a Story

1

2

4

3

Stephanie LaBaff
Illustrated by Tom LaBaff

Enslow Elementary
an imprint of
Enslow Publishers, Inc.

E 40 Industrial Road
Box 398
Berkeley Heights, NJ 07922
USA

http://www.enslow.com

Enslow Elementary, an imprint of Enslow Publishers, Inc.

Enslow Elementary® is a registered trademark of Enslow Publishers, Inc.

Library of Congress Cataloging-in-Publication Data
LaBaff, Stephanie.
  Draw animals in 4 easy steps : then write a story / by Stephanie LaBaff ;
illustrated by Tom LaBaff.
      p. cm. — (Drawing in 4 easy steps)
  Includes bibliographical references and index.
  Summary: "Learn to draw animals and write a story about them, with a story example and story prompts"—Provided by publisher.
  ISBN 978-0-7660-3840-0
  1. Animals in art—Juvenile literature. 2. Drawing—Technique—Juvenile literature. 3. Animals—Juvenile literature. 4. Authorship—Juvenile literature. I. LaBaff, Tom. II. Title. III. Title: Draw animals in four easy steps.
  NC780.L23 2012
  743.6—dc22
                          2011012130
Paperback ISBN 978-1-4644-0013-1
ePUB ISBN 978-1-4645-0460-0
PDF ISBN 978-1-4646-0460-7

Printed in the United States of America

092011 Lake Book Manufacturing, Inc., Melrose Park, IL

10 9 8 7 6 5 4 3 2 1

Illustration Credits: Tom LaBaff

To Our Readers: We have done our best to make sure all Internet Addresses in this book were active and appropriate when we went to press. However, the author and the publisher have no control over and assume no liability for the material available on those Internet sites or on other Web sites they may link to. Any comments or suggestions can be sent by e-mail to comments@enslow.com or to the address on the back cover.

♻ Enslow Publishers, Inc., is committed to printing our books on recycled paper. The paper in every book contains 10% to 30% post-consumer waste (PCW). The cover board on the outside of each book contains 100% PCW. Our goal is to do our part to help young people and the environment too!

Contents

Getting Started

Lots of Paper

Pencil sharpener

your imagination

Pencil

Eraser

ARTIST'S SURVIVAL KIT

Drawing animals is as easy as 1, 2, 3, 4! Follow the 4 steps for each picture in this book. You will be amazed at what you can draw. After some practice, you will be able to make your own adjustments, too. Change a pose, move a leg, or draw a different animal. There are lots of possibilities!

Follow the 4 Steps

1 Start with big shapes, such as the head and body.

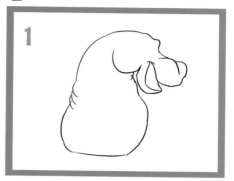

2 Add smaller shapes, such as the arms and legs. In each step, new lines are shown in red.

3 Continue adding new lines. Erase lines as needed.

4 Add final details and color. Your animal will come to life!

Cat

1

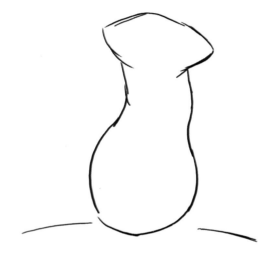

2

3

Erase the dotted lines behind the legs.

4

Great Dane

1

2

3

Erase the dotted line behind the right leg.

Don't forget the other eye!

4

Goldfish

1

Start with a lemon shape.

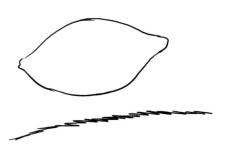

2

3

We can see through the fins, so you don't need to erase behind them.

4

Parakeet

1

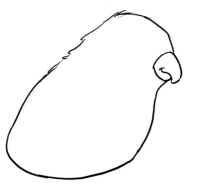

2

3

Now the hard part—the feet. Take your time. Erase the dotted line behind the tail feathers.

4

Dachshund

1

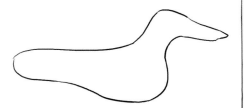

2

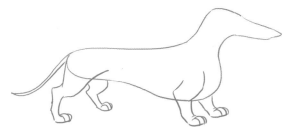

3

Erase the dotted lines behind the back leg, ear, collar, and front leg.

4

Elephant

1

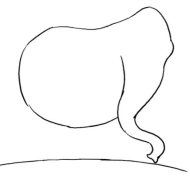

2

3

Erase the dotted lines behind the ear and leg.

4

Add a line to the ear.

Tasmanian Devil

1

2

3

Erase the dotted lines behind the ear, and the front and back legs.

4

Lion

1

2

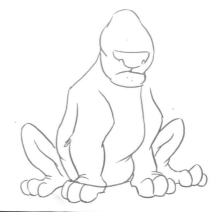

3

Go wild with the hair!

Erase the dotted line behind the paw.

4

Snake

1

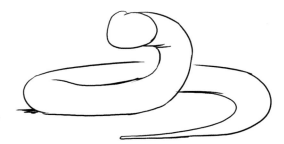

2

3

Add shadows to make it look like the snake is on the ground.

4

Gorilla

1

2

3

Erase the dotted line behind the arm.

Don't worry about the detail on the feet.

4

Koala

1

2

3

Erase the dotted lines behind the arms and hands.

4

Hippopotamus

1

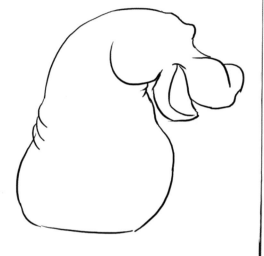

2

3

Erase the
dotted line
behind the
leg.

4

Kangaroo

1

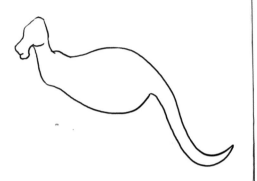

2

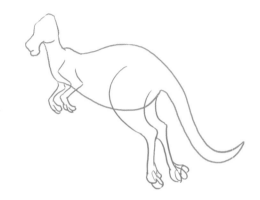

3

Add a smile.

Erase the dotted lines behind the leg, arm, and pouch.

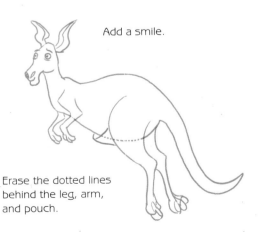

4

Sugar Glider

1

2

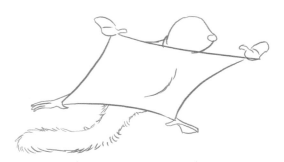

3 Erase the dotted line across the neck.

4

Giraffe

1

2

3

Show an open mouth by erasing the line.

Erase the dotted lines behind its legs.

4

Pig

3

Erase the dotted lines behind the leg.

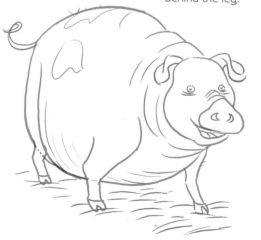

4

Chicken

1

2

3

Erase the dotted lines under the beak, and behind the wattle, legs, and wing.

4

Donkey

1

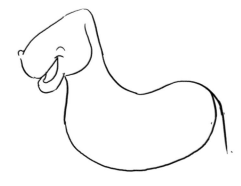

2

3

Erase the dotted lines behind the legs.

4

23

Cow

1

2

3

4

Give her some grass.
She's hungry!

Sheep

1

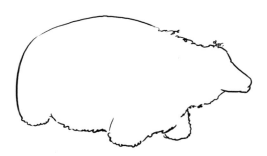

2

3

4

Dolphin

1

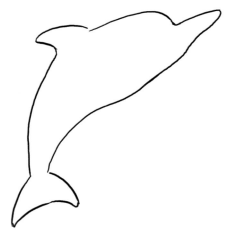

2

3

Just add water!

4

Turtle

1

2

3

Erase the dotted lines behind the flipper and neck area.

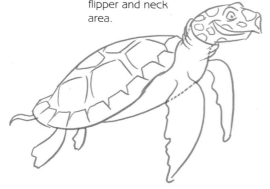

4

Seal

1

2

3

Erase the dotted line behind the flippers.

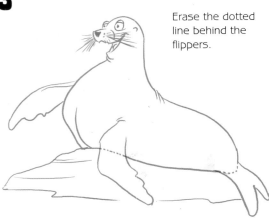

4

Killer Whale

1

2

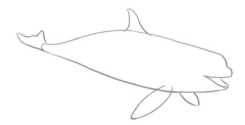

3

Erase the dotted lines behind the fin and flippers.

Add a line to show where the sea floor is.

4

Manatee

1

2

3

Erase the dotted line behind the flipper.

Add some minnows.

4

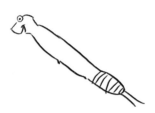

Butterfly

1

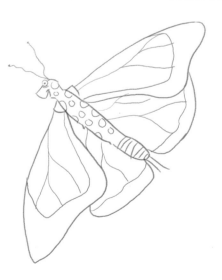

2

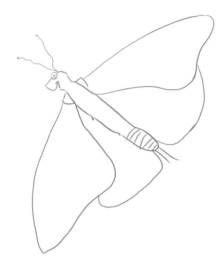

3

4

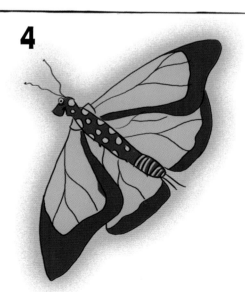

Chipmunk

1

2

3

Erase the dotted lines behind the front leg.

4

Salamander

1

2

3

Erase the dotted line behind the front leg and tail.

4

Sparrow

1

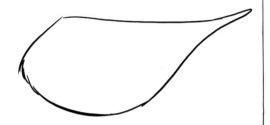

2

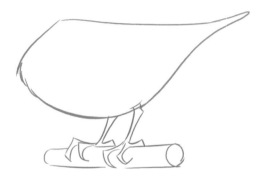

3

Erase the dotted lines behind the neck and leg.

4

Racoon

1

2

3

Erase the dotted lines behind the ear and leg.

4

How to Write a Story

Write a Story in 5 Easy Steps

Are you ready to write a story to go with your drawings? Maybe you have a story you want to illustrate. Follow these five simple steps to make your very own story with drawings.

Step 1: *Prewriting*

Do you want to write about animals? Maybe you have an idea for a story about animals in the jungle. Keep in mind the drawings you want to use and base your story around them.

One way to begin your story is to answer these questions: Who? What? Why? Where? When? How?
For example:
What is your animal?
What happens to it in your story?
Why is its story interesting?
Where and when does it live?
How does it find food?

Who? What?
How? Why?
When? Where?

Here is a good brainstorming exercise:
Fold a paper into six columns. Write the
words *Who? What? Why? Where? When?*
and *How?* at the top of each column.
Write down every answer that comes into
your head in the matching column. Do this
for about five or ten minutes. Take a look
at your list and pick out the ideas that you
like the best. Now you are ready to write
your story.

Animal Story Starters:

The salamander hid in the leaves and
watched . . .

The seal was frolicking in the water near
the rocks. . . .

A herd of elephants stampeded through
the forest. . . .

The sugar glider soared over the
treetops searching for . . .

All of the animals were quiet in the barn
when all of the sudden . . .

The goldfish watched from his bowl as
the cat paced outside the window. . . .

Step 2: Writing

Use the ideas from the list you made in Step 1. Write your story all the way through. Don't stop to make changes. You can always make changes later.

A story about a gorilla eating bananas isn't very interesting. What could happen to this gorilla? What if there was a lion getting ready to pounce on the gorilla? Think of all the trouble the gorilla could cause while trying to escape. Your story will be more exciting if you don't make things too easy for the gorilla.

Step 3: Editing

Read your story. Is there a way to make it better? Rewrite the parts that you can improve. You might want to ask a friend or teacher to help. Ask them for their ideas.

Step 4: Proofreading

Make sure the spelling, punctuation, and grammar are correct.

Storyboarding

Check to see that your story works with your drawings. Find a table or other flat surface. Spread your drawings out in the order that goes with your story. Then place the matching text below each drawing. When you have your story the way you like it, go to Step 5. You can pick a way to publish your story.

Step 5: Publishing Your Book

You can make your story into a book. There are many different forms your book can take. Here are a few ideas:

🐾 Simple book—Staple sheets of blank paper together along their edges.

🐾 Folded book—Fold sheets of blank paper in half, then staple on the fold.

🐾 Hardcover book—Buy a blank hardcover book. Then write your finished story in the book, leaving spaces to add your art.

🐾 Bound book—Punch a few holes along the edges of some pieces of paper. Tie them up or fill the holes with paper fasteners. There are many fun and colorful binding options at office supply stores.

🐾 Digital book—Create a digital book using your computer. There are some great programs available. Ask an adult to help you find one that is right for you.

Our Story

You have finished the five steps of writing and illustrating a story. We bet you created a great story! Want to see ours? Turn the page and take a peek.

Sugar Glider's New Friend

One night, a sugar glider soared through the air looking for something to eat. Down below, he spotted a group of Tasmanian devils playing with a white ball. They laughed as they rolled it back and forth.

Sugar landed in a nearby tree and sighed. "I wish I had a friend to play with," the lonely little glider thought. He knew he couldn't join the devils. They would have him for their dinner!

Suddenly Sugar heard a loud "crack!" He looked down and saw that the white ball now had a large crack down one side. A moment later, the ball began to move back and forth! The startled devils quickly ran off into the woods.

After making sure the coast was clear, Sugar hurried over to the white ball. Carefully, he inched closer. Suddenly he heard another large crack. Out popped a tiny head! Sugar gasped. It was a baby sea turtle! He stared as the turtle slowly broke his way out of his shell. The two creatures looked at each other.

"Hi, I'm Sugar," the glider said. "Would you like to play?"

The tiny turtle looked doubtful. "I know I was just born, but I don't think I'm supposed to be friends with you." And he turned and started walking toward the sea.

Sadly, the glider watched him go. But before the turtle could get very far, Sugar heard a rustling noise coming from the woods. He looked behind him. The Tasmanian devils were back! He quickly climbed the nearest tree. Safely hidden, he watched as the devils headed straight for the baby turtle.

"Oh, no!" Sugar thought. "He'll never make it. I've got to help him!" Just as the devils were about to reach the turtle, Sugar swooped down and grabbed the turtle.

They glided their way to the beach, where Sugar gently placed the turtle back on the ground.

"You saved my life!" said the turtle. "I'm sorry I said I wouldn't be your friend. Do you forgive me?" "Of course," said Sugar. "That's what friends are for!" The two laughed and ran off down the beach, playing happily in the sand.

Further Reading

Books

Brecke, Nicole, and Patricia M. Stockland. Horses You Can Draw. Minneapolis, Minn.: Millbrook Press, 2010.

Green, Dan. How to Draw 101 Animals. Woodbridge, Suffolk, UK: Top That! Publishing Place, 2004.

Hart, Christopher. Cartoon Cute Animals: How to Draw the Most Irresistible Creatures on the Planet. New York: Watson-Guptill Publications, 2010.

Leaf, Munro. The Story of Ferdinand. New York: Viking Children's Books, 2011.

Steig, William. Amos & Boris. New York: Square Fish, 2009.

Internet Addresses

PBS Kids. Dot's Story Factory.
<http://pbskids.org/storyfactory/story.html>

Scholastic.com. Writing Games.
<http://www.scholastic.com/kids/stacks/games/>

Index

B

brainstorming, 37
butterfly, 31

C

cat, 6
chicken, 22
chipmunk, 32
cow, 24

D

dachshund, 10
dolphin, 26
donkey, 23

E

editing, 41
elephant, 11

G

giraffe, 20
goldfish, 8
gorilla, 15
Great Dane, 7

H

hippo, 17

K

kangaroo, 18
killer whale, 29
koala, 16

L

lion, 13

M

manatee, 30

P

parakeet, 9
pig, 21
prewriting, 36
proofreading, 41
publishing, 42

R

raccoon, 35

S

salamander, 33
seal, 28
sheep, 25
snake, 14
sparrow, 34
story starters, 39
storyboarding, 41
sugar glider, 19

T

Tazmanian devil,
   12
turtle, 27

W

writing, 40